Patterns
of
Prayer

PATTERNS OF PRAYER

Eugene McCaffrey, O.C.D.

 PAULIST PRESS New York/Mahwah, New Jersey

Cover design by Valerie Petro

Book design by Joseph E. Petta

Copyright © 2003 by Eugene McCaffrey

Library of Congress Cataloging-in-Publication Data

McCaffrey, Eugene.
Patterns of prayer / Eugene McCaffrey.
p.   cm.
ISBN 0-8091-4113-2
1. Prayer—Christianity. I. Title.
BV215 .M375 2002
248.3′2—dc21
2002151066

Published by Paulist Press
997 Macarthur Boulevard
Mahwah, New Jersey 07430

www.paulistpress.com

Printed and bound in Canada

First published by Darlington Carmel, England, 1992

Contents

Getting Started

With so many things in life, getting started is often the hardest part. Prayer is no exception. Yet even "the journey of a thousand miles begins with the first step." And it is that first step that matters most, at least in prayer. The only way to begin to pray is to begin.

These pages were written simply to help people get started. They were originally written as prayer leaflets—loose, easy-to-hold pages that could be carried in a handbag or pocket and read at odd moments throughout the day. They are more concerned with praying than with prayer. There is no attempt to convince anyone about the importance or value of prayer. They are offered as an invitation to pray or as an encouragement to keep on doing so.

Perhaps encouragement is what we all need most in prayer. Most people want to pray and are, in fact, praying far better and more often than they realize. But what is happening in their lives does not seem to fit in to the standard definitions of prayer! It's easy to be discouraged by the way others talk or write about prayer. Indeed, some of the saints had the same experience: "I had to leave aside the learned books," St. Thérèse of Lisieux, the Little Flower, tells us, "and simply talk to God in my own way, as a child talks to its father."[1]

Prayer is simple but it is not easy. It is simple because God loves each one of us personally and uniquely, and prayer is basically our response to that love. But it is not easy because we ourselves complicate it and turn it into something it was never meant to be. We can make too much of prayer as being something special, as if it were different from the rest of our lives, from the way we feel, the joys we share and the pain and struggle of everyday life. Real prayer is as real as the life we live, and the one cannot be separated from the other.

The one condition essential to prayer is desire: to want to pray is the beginning of prayer. Without it, we will never even make a start; with it, we have already begun. Wanting to pray becomes much easier if we realize how much God himself wants it and invites us to do so: "No matter how much you think you are searching for God," St. John of the Cross, Doctor of the Church, reminds us, "he is looking for you much more."[2] God's prayer is for us to seek him; our prayers must be to stop hiding from him.

We must never lose a prayer or let it die because we cannot find words to express it, for prayer is always greater than words. Each prayer is special and unique and if we do not pray our own prayer, no one ever will; it will be lost forever. We can never pray in the wrong way as long as we pray in our own way. There is a prayer hidden within every human heart waiting to be set free. If we listen, we can hear it ourselves, and even if we don't, we know that God already does.

The one thing we must never do is measure our prayers. Long or short prayers are not the issue; length of time is not as important as taking time. The heart of prayer is to try to say what we mean and mean what we say. If the heart is right, the prayer cannot be wrong.

Because the chapters were written individually and over the space of a few years, some points in the book are repeated under different headings. This only serves to underline the original purpose for which they were written: a gentle reminder of the presence of God in our lives and an invitation to linger awhile and rest in that presence. Perhaps, even in book form, they are still best read in that way.

DISCOVERING PRAYER

God, in all that is most living and incarnate in Him, is not far away from us, altogether apart from the world we see, touch, hear, smell and taste about us. Rather He awaits us every instant in our action, in the work of the moment. There is a sense in which He is at the tip of my pen, my spade, my brush, my needle – of my heart and of my thought.

—St. Thérèse of Lisieux[3]

You cannot teach anyone to pray, just as you cannot teach anyone to love. Both must be discovered within.

We don't learn to pray the way we learn a language, through grammars and textbooks. For prayer is knowledge not of a thing, but of a Person. It is not so much something we learn as something we become, something we already are. It is growth in relationship, in living, loving intimacy with a friend.

Prayer is more a discovery than a task, more an adventure than a duty. It is a wish turned Godward, an unveiling of ourselves before him. It makes a pilgrim out of a wanderer.

Learning about God

Learning to pray is first of all learning about God: who he is, what he has told us about himself and about his love for us. Real prayer always starts with God. For us, prayer is a response.

How we approach God in prayer very much depends on our attitude toward him. If God is for us a Father and a friend, someone near to us, then our prayer will be childlike, warm and tender. If on the other hand he is for us a God of wrath and anger, a policeman and a judge, then our prayer can only be cold and distant, nothing but a burden and a duty.

Learning about Ourselves

Learning to pray also means learning about ourselves: who we are, what we have received, what we can become. To pray is to release the infinite possibilities hidden within every human heart. To know ourselves as God knows us, to realize how we have been gifted by nature and grace, is to break out automatically into prayer.

Prayer is a gift—one we have already received. Hidden within the heart of every Christian, given along with the gift of faith, is the power to pray. "Prayer," wrote St. Gregory of Sinai, the 14th-century mystic, "is the manifestation of Baptism."[4] We don't pray just to become holy; we pray because we *are* holy. "Become what you are" is a basic principle of prayer and the ideal in our whole relationship with God.

Prayer of the Heart

There are times in our lives when we can't help praying, when prayer springs spontaneously from our heart: times of crisis and fear, when we automatically call out for help; times, too, of joy and happiness when we feel the need just to say "thank you" to someone. But prayer is not only for these special moments. It is the leaven of life, our everyday food and drink. Prayer and life go hand in hand; the heartbeat of prayer is our daily living. Prayer reflects life, gathering it into a unity, giving it voice. Life, in turn, tests our prayer and gives it depth. Thus we pray as we live; we become what we pray.

Gospel Prayers

Some people think that prayer is only for the perfect—a way of the saints. Certainly this is not the gospel teaching. The prayers that touched the heart of Christ were the prayers of ordinary simple folk, sinners most of them, like ourselves—the sick, the blind, the lepers, lost sheep and prodigal sons: "Lord, have mercy," "Lord, have pity"; they were prayers of need, made in faith and trust.

For St. Teresa of Avila, the 16th-century Spanish mystic, prayer is a "royal road."[5] In her time, many roads were toll roads or had restricted access. The King's road, however, was an open highway, free and accessible to all, a road for saints and sinners alike. For Teresa, prayer is the Lord's own highway leading directly to his presence.

There is nothing professional about prayer. The only expert is the one who prays. This is beautifully expressed in a phrase attributed to St. John Climacus, monk of Mount Sinai: "Prayer is God's gift to those who pray." It is a path that opens up only to those who walk along it. The most important disposition for prayer is to want to get in touch with God. To want to pray is in itself already a prayer.

Pray as You Can

Too many people fret and worry over ways and methods of praying. Ultimately, there is only one way to pray—*your* way. Nothing is so personal as prayer and it should be as unique and special as the one who prays. There are as many ways of praying as there are people who pray. Prayer, like the way you talk or the way you walk, should be uniquely yours. "No two people," St. John of the Cross reminds us, "walk more than half way on the same road to God."[6] Each one has his or her own secret passageway to God and must have the courage to find it. Of nothing in life so much as prayer should we be able to say, "I did it my way."

We can spend a lot of time measuring our prayer and judging our progress. Yet prayer in itself is not the barometer of prayer. The only measuring rod of prayer is love and our willingness to share that love with others. Often when our prayer seems poorest in our own eyes, it may be the most precious in the eyes of God.

It is essential to realize, St. Teresa remarks, that God does not lead us all along the same road.[7] It may be that someone who thinks himself/herself as going along the lowest road of all is the highest in the sight of God.

Sometimes it is more important to pray than to pray well, more acceptable to God that we just *try* to pray than that we actually realize we are doing so.

In the whole world of prayer, the practical advice of the Benedictine author, Dom John

Chapman, holds true: "Pray as you can, not as you can't."[8] In other words, pray as you are, not as you wish you were; pray where you are, not from where you think you should be; pray as you can, and not the way others have told you to.

The Heart of Prayer

Perhaps the most wonderful thing of all to remember about prayer is that God *wants* us to pray. He sends out the invitations, the door is open, the way prepared. If prayer is a dialogue, it is because God has already spoken and has said, Come, I need your love. In prayer the heart is more important than the lips, the attitude of mind speaks louder than the words we use. It is the prayer behind the "prayers" that matters, the unspoken prayer that only God can hear. Talking to God is not the same as talking about him; finding him yourself is very different from hearing about him from others.

Prayer, then, is more than words. It is sharing—sharing your life with God. It is friendship—God and you together. Above all it is love—first discovering his love for you, and then your response. Prayer is saying "yes" to God. And to God who has everything, it is the one thing that is ours to give. "For me," said St. Thérèse of Lisieux, "prayer means launching out of the heart towards God; it means lifting up one's eyes, quite simply, to heaven, a cry of grateful love, from the crest of joy or the trough of despair."[9]

Someone has rightly said that our lives are different from the day we discover prayer not as a last resort, but as a first resort.

PRAYER AND PRESENCE

God, in all that is most living and incarnate in Him, is not far away from us altogether apart from the world about us we see, touch, hear, smell and taste. Rather, He awaits us at every instant in our action, in the work of the moment. There is a sense in which He is at the tip of my pen, my spade, my brush, my needle—of my heart and of my thought.[10]

—Pierre Teilhard de Chardin

There is an old Portuguese proverb that says, "When God wants to hide something he places it right in front of our eyes." Perhaps nowhere is this truth more clearly shown than in the mystery of his own presence in the world. God's presence is a hidden presence—but only for those who do not wish to see.

All religion, all spirituality is in a way a response to, or an awareness of, God's presence in our lives. Religion is essentially the meeting place of God and humanity, a meeting that takes place here and now in this world of ours, a world he has created and one charged with the grandeur of his presence.

There is no time, no place in our daily lives in which God is not present. There are not even certain times or places where he is *more* present. God is always the same. He does not "come" and "go" from one place to another. Everywhere and at all times he is wholly and totally present to everything that exists.

God's Footprints

Perhaps the most important thing to remember about God's presence in the world is that it is not an impersonal force or energy exercising its influence from some remote region of outer space. His influence is supremely personal and immediate. Because he made all things out of nothing, he is continually present to his own creation, distilling existence from moment to moment. It is only through this presence and power that the world continues to exist and that all created things continue to live and grow: "In him we live and move and have our being" (Acts 17:28).

Creation is one way in which God reveals himself to us. He speaks to us in the delicate beauty of a snowdrop or the awesome majesty of the soaring mountains. Sometimes we can glimpse his presence in the setting sun or sense his voice in the silence of the sea or in the gentle whisper of an evening breeze: "The heavens are telling the glory of God; and the firmament proclaims His handiwork" (Ps 19:1).

14

The saints have always understood this. St. Francis of Assisi celebrated it in the *Canticle of the Sun*; St. John of the Cross spoke of creation bearing the footprints of God as "he passed by in haste, scattering a thousand graces, clothing it in beauty."[11]

Perhaps one of the most beautiful expressions of this is found in the writings of the 14th-century English mystic, Julian of Norwich:

> He showed me a little thing, the size of a hazelnut, in the palm of my hand, and it was as round as a ball. I looked at it with my mind's eye and I thought, "What can this be?" And the answer came, "It is all that is made." I marveled that it could last, for I thought it might have crumbled to nothing, it was so small. And the answer came to me again, "It lasts and ever shall last because God loves it, for all things have being through the love of God." In this little thing, then, I saw three truths. The first is that God made it. The second is that God loves it. The third is that God looks after it.[12]

A Personal Presence

The supreme point to remember is that God's presence is personal simply because he himself is a person. He is not the "ground of our being" in some dry, remote sort of way. We are not "surrounded" by God as by air, light or energy—like a fish in the ocean or a bird in the sky. God is a personal God and that is how he has revealed himself; he knows us personally, loves us individually, cares for us uniquely. His eyes are loving and his care is special: "I have called you by name, you are mine" (Isa 43:1); "I have inscribed you on the palm of my hand" (Isa 49:16).

Personal presence is different from physical or material presence. Personal presence is characterized by knowledge and love, by communication and sharing. A casual "good morning" or a brief business call does not establish personal presence. I can be more present to a friend on the telephone than to a stranger on a crowded bus. When lovers meet, the relationship is dynamic and they both respond creatively to the presence of the other. So it is with God's presence. He is not just physically present to me; he is present to me in love, friendship and sharing.

Though God is present to all created things, it is only the human spirit that can respond to him. Only the human heart has the power and privilege of being aware of God's presence. We have the potential to know God in a personal way, to love him and to live consciously in his presence. This is the core of the religious experience and the starting point of all spirituality. It is also the beginning and source of prayer. All prayer is in some way a response to the mystery of God's presence in our lives. It is a journey into presence.

A Presence Within

Yet God is not just present to us, no matter how personal and immediate that may be; he is also present *within* us. By a special and beautiful gift we call "grace," he has made the human heart his own dwelling place on earth. This presence is pure gift and pure love. Through it, God dwells in the human heart as in a home. It was the great promise made at the Last Supper and fulfilled at Pentecost: "Those who love me will keep my word, and my Father will love them, and we will come to them and make our home with them" (John 14:23). This presence we call an "indwelling" presence, because God makes the human heart his own dwelling place on earth. He comes as a friend seeking friendship and as a lover seeking a response of love. It is a dynamic presence. It calls us to awareness and response. Above all, it is a loving presence and love by its very nature is creative. It is an invitation to share the very life of God, present within, or as St. Paul puts it, "to to be holy and blameless before him in love" (Eph 1:4).

Prayer and Presence

It is this presence that gives its distinctive quality to Christian prayer and gives meaning to the practice of "living in the presence of God." Living in his presence has nothing to do with having a good memory or with some sort of mental gymnastics. It is more a question of awareness and attention. It comes from the realization that God is close—"closer to me than my inmost self" is how St. Augustine expressed it[13]—and that to find him I have only to look within my own heart. Few have understood or expressed this truth better than the 17th-century French Carmelite, Brother Lawrence of the Resurrection. For him, practice of the presence of God was a way of life as much as a way of prayer:

18

> I have given up all non-obligatory
> devotions and prayers and concen-
> trate on being always in His holy pres-
> ence; I keep myself in His presence by
> simple attentiveness and a loving
> gaze upon God....As for time formally
> set aside for prayer, it is only a contin-
> uation of this same exercise.[14]

The first principle of prayer is that God is open and accessible. He knows me, not from a distance, but from within. Prayer is sharing that presence. It is a meeting of two presences. Indeed, a good description of prayer is "being present to Presence." In prayer we don't have to make God present. We have only to be aware that he is there, within what St. Teresa calls the "heaven of the soul,"[15] or what Brother Lawrence refers to as "the oratory of the heart."[16]

When Jesus told his disciples to "pray always" (Luke 18:1), he was not asking the impossible. He was not talking about "saying" prayers as such, but about prayer as a way of life. To live a full Christian life is to live constantly in the presence of God, and that is just another way of making a prayer out of life itself. It is not a duty one is forced to perform, but a Christian birthright.

A saintly monk once went on a pilgrimage to a sacred shrine. As he approached the town, he lay down tired and exhausted at the side of the road to rest. He was rudely awakened by another pilgrim who told him it was time to pray and that he should turn his face towards the shrine. "I will indeed," replied the monk, "but first do me the honor of turning my feet where they will not be pointing to God!"

PRAYER AS LISTENING

Do you imagine that God is silent because we cannot hear him? He speaks directly to our hearts when from our hearts we ask him to do so.
—St. Teresa of Avila[17]

A lot of people start their prayers at the wrong end. They begin with themselves instead of with God. Real prayer always starts with God—with his love for us and his invitation to friendship. No matter how much we think we want God, he always wants us much more.

The first principle of prayer is that God is accessible. He is not some vague, distant shadow out in the unknown. Out of the darkness and the void, God has come and told us about himself. Just as friends and lovers share secrets, God has shared his secret with us: the secret that he is Love and that we are called to share it. All that is needed is a "listening heart" to hear that message of love. How well Solomon understood this need when, in his search for wisdom, he prayed for the gift of hearing and understanding: "Give your servant an understanding mind" (1 Kgs 3:9).

First Love

Prayer always begins with God because he first loved us. This is the whole meaning of the Bible story, from the opening pages of *Genesis* to the *Book of Revelation.* It is the message of the first Christmas, just as it is of Calvary: God with us, God near us, laying down his life and taking it up again for us, proving his love in life and in death.

Most people think of prayer as asking something of God, forgetting that he already gave us everything when he gave us his Son: "Long ago God spoke to our ancestors in many and various ways...but in these last days he has spoken to us by a Son" (Heb 1:1–2). Jesus is God's "I love you" to the world—the supreme gift "in whom are hidden all the treasures of wisdom and knowledge" (Col 2:3). In giving us his Son, God has given us everything: even though God is infinite, he has no more to give. The message proclaimed by God at the transfiguration and the response he wants from us are still the same: "This is my Son, the Beloved; listen to him!" (Mark 9:7).

Blessed Are Those Who Listen

In the scriptures, listening always takes precedence over seeing. The ear is more important than the eye. Faith comes from what is heard, St. Paul reminds us (Rom 10:14). Jesus opens his teaching with the simple admonition, "Listen!" (Mark 4:3). He ends with the invitation, "Let anyone with ears to hear listen!" (Mark 4:9).

The first and the greatest commandment is the commandment to love God. Yet it is a commandment dependent upon listening: "Hear, O Israel: The Lord is our God, the Lord alone. You shall love the Lord your God with all your heart...." (Deut 6:4–5). To love is to listen, really to hear and to receive. As Mary of Bethany discovered, sitting at the feet of the Lord, the "better part" (Luke 10:42) is often just this openness and this listening. Jesus himself counted it among the beatitudes: "Blessed are those who hear the word of God and obey it" (Luke 11:28). When one really loves, listening is every bit as important as speaking; hearing the word is just as precious as talking about it. Prayer begins when we receive the word of God with a welcoming heart and let it take root in our souls.

Invitation

How often we think of prayer as knocking at the door of heaven when, in fact, it is the other way around. It is God who is doing the knocking: "Listen! I am standing at the door, knocking; if you hear my voice and open the door, I will come in to you and eat with you, and you with me" (Rev 3:20). For the truth is that God is always knocking, always speaking, always inviting. All he asks is that we listen to his voice and open the door to him. The rest will follow: as we "dine" with him, we grow in the knowledge and love of him. The beginning of prayer is to let God into our lives and to open the door of our hearts to him. How well Mother Teresa of Calcutta expressed this truth when she said, "Prayer enlarges the heart until it is capable of containing God's gift of himself."[18]

To Pray Is to Listen

It takes two to pray, each giving and each receiving. To receive is just as important as to give. Listening is a way of receiving. In prayer we must listen to God just as, in the same way, we ask him to listen to us. That is why prayer always implies an openness to God, a placing of ourselves at his disposal and a readiness to receive. Watching and waiting are the eyes of prayer; a listening heart is the key that unlocks the door. Prayer is talking to someone who is listening, and listening to someone who is talking.

God speaks to us in many ways: in the scriptures, in the liturgy, in the community, in the wonders of creation, in the circumstances of daily life and in the depths of our own heart. His voice has many sounds and it often rings in strange places. Our needs, our friends, the people we meet, the joys and sorrows of life—all these can carry his message and speak to us of his love. To pray is to listen. To pray well is to listen deeply—to God, to ourselves and to others.

Sharing His Presence

Speech implies presence. Where God acts he is immediately present. His word is a creative word. He spoke and all things were made, and he is always totally present to his own creation. God does not come and go from place to place. To speak of placing ourselves in his presence can be misleading. We cannot, in fact, place ourselves outside of it;

we are surrounded by it as by the air we breathe. "Closer to me," St. Augustine tells us, "than my inmost self."[19]

To pray is to realize this presence of God, for prayer is not so much talking to God as sharing his presence. It is a meeting of presences: God's presence to me, my presence to him. It is a way of being open and receptive to his presence. Listening sharpens awareness. To listen to him is to find him; to hear his voice is to come into his presence. Listening to God's voice, hearing his word, is at the same time being aware of his presence. And what is prayer, ultimately, but our response to this presence?

Silence

Silence is an essential condition for listening. Prayer is born in silence, a still receptive silence that enables one to hear the deep vibrations of the spirit. Silence is our way of helping God so that he can help us. We try to be still, conscious of our own poverty and of our own need to hear and to receive. Silence is much more than an absence of words or noise, much more even than just being quiet. Rather, it is a response of our whole being reaching out to grasp the word of life. It is an alert and attentive receptiveness to "hear the word of God and obey it" (Luke 11:28). Like the boy Samuel, we cry out with our whole heart, "Speak, for your servant is listening" (1 Sam 3:10).

Listening Heart

We often complain that God does not hear our prayers, does not listen to our requests, and that when we speak he does not listen. Yet frequently the truth is the other way around. It is we who do not hear, we who are deaf to his requests, insensitive to the pleadings of his love. Too often our hearts are set for transmission only, and incoming calls are not received. His invitation is not accepted. We do not respond because we do not listen; we forget that for us prayer is always the response of a listening heart. Yet the truth remains: God is always "on the air" and it takes only a listening heart to hear his voice and understand the message he speaks.

CONTEMPLATIVE MEDITATION

Meditation is not just a way of "doing" something but it is a way of "becoming" someone—becoming yourself: created by God, redeemed by Jesus and a temple of the Holy Spirit....In meditation we go beyond thoughts, even holy thoughts. Meditation is concerned not so much with thinking as with being. And in contemplative prayer we seek to become the person we are called to be: not by thinking about God but by being with Him.[20]

—John Main, O.S.B.

There are many ways of praying, just as there are many ways of living. Contemplative meditation is both a way of prayer and a way of life. It is one particular response in faith to the reality of God's presence in the world. It is neither difficult nor mysterious. Rather, it is the natural response of a child of God who turns to his Father in simplicity and love. It is a prayer of confidence, based on the gospel promise, "Those who love me will keep my word, and my Father will love them, and we will come to them and make our home with them" (John 14:23). It takes as its starting point our Lord's assurance that there is no need to use many words in prayer: "…your Father knows what you need before you ask him" (Matt 6:7–8).

To Pray Is to Love

In general, to contemplate means to look. In prayer this looking is neither physical nor intellectual. It is a looking in faith and in love. A living faith and a loving heart are the very breath of all true contemplative prayer. In prayer, St. Teresa reminds us, "the important thing is not to think much, but to love much."[21] Prayer is not just having nice thoughts about God or experiencing fine feelings or emotions. Rather, it is a being with him in faith and a looking towards him in love: an entering into the mystery of a real and personal God in whose love we share.

In the same way, to meditate means to think, to reflect or to ponder. But the meditation we are concerned with here is not a mere thinking process, with God as the end result. Rather, it is a deep, prayerful attentiveness by which we get in touch with our own inner selves, so that we can be more open to God who is within. The word, "meditation" comes from the Latin *stare in medio,* to stand or abide in the center. The centering is not on ourselves, but on God. This loving and attentive pondering on God and on his word is what the Desert Fathers call "the prayer of the heart": the prayer of the whole person standing before God with the "head in the heart."

Contemplative meditation, then, is a way of prayer and a way of love. In contemplative meditation, loving is more important than thinking, listening more important than asking, being more important than doing, and a deep and attentive silence the most important of all.

Who Prays?

In prayer we reach out to God as he is in himself. But it is sometimes helpful, perhaps even essential, to step back a little so as first of all to find ourselves. After all, it is the "me" who prays—the whole person, body as well as soul, and not just some part of me—mind or will or head. Sometimes distractions and difficulties in prayer come from forgetting the obvious fact that we are not angels, but men and women of flesh and blood. It is not just that I have a body. Rather, I *am* a body. I am a unity made up of both body and soul: a spiritual body and an incarnate soul.

Nor is it sufficient to say that I "use" my body in prayer. No, the body itself prays. It is part of my total response to God, the visible expression of the hidden workings of grace in my soul. When I stand before God in prayer, my body too has a right to stand with me in prayer and worship. Just as the body is the principal way in which I communicate with others, and is itself part of the communication, so too in prayer it can and should be part of my communication with God.

Respect and reverence for the body is a deeply Christian thing, a natural consequence of belief in the goodness of all God's creation and of its sanctification in Christ through the mystery of the incarnation. "Or do you know that your body is a temple of the Holy Spirit," St. Paul reminds the Corinthians, so "glorify God in your body" (1 Cor 6:19–20). With good reason, then, we emphasize the total involvement of the body in prayer, especially contemplative prayer. Such things as breathing, relaxation, sensory awareness and bodily posture play an important part in helping me to love God not just with mind and soul, but with body and heart as well. They help me not only to appreciate, but even to *create* the stillness and silence essential for prayer, to be more present to myself so that I can be more open to God, to be more aware not only of who God is, but of who I am. When I pray with my body, I put body into my prayer.

Presence

Contemplative meditation is essentially a prayer of presence. It is in this sense that prayer has been described as "being present to Presence." In prayer we do not have to make God present. He is not "here" or "there." He is one, unique and indivisible, and through creation he has communicated his presence to all things: "In him we live and move and have our being" (Acts 17:28). The glory of our human nature is that we can consciously reflect, and lovingly respond to, this self-communicating presence of God. And this, not only to him as the Creator-God who holds all things in being by his power and his knowledge, but as a friend and a Father who comes to dwell within as "the sweet Guest of the soul."

There are many kinds of presence and different ways of responding to each. Among friends, the nature of presence depends on the quality of love, and God's presence is no exception. I can be more present to a friend on the telephone or while writing a letter than to a total stranger who is sitting beside me on the train. As in human friendships, so also in divine: it is the quality of the relationship that determines the presence. With God there is both physical presence and a relationship of personal love and friendship. He is totally present to me in love; he loves me unconditionally and without distraction. His invitation is for me to share this presence in faith and in love—to be present to him through awareness, attentive listening and loving attention. Prayer, and especially contemplative meditation, is my response to this personal self-giving of God in love. "However quietly we speak, he is so near that he will hear us," St. Teresa reminds us. "We need no wings to go in search of him, but have only to find a place where we can be alone and look at him present within us."[22]

Awareness

Awareness is the quality of my presence to someone or something. It is the art of letting the thoughts flow around a particular idea or image, looking at something actively but without words. Being a state of wakefulness and attentiveness, it is the very opposite of a stare or a drifting into an objectless void. Rather, it is an active attentiveness and a loving concentration on one particular aspect of reality here and now present. Awareness is always concerned with the present moment and the concrete reality of its immediate experience. It is the "one-pointedness" of which the Zen mystics speak, the "single-mindedness" of the 14th-century classic, *The Cloud of Unknowing,* the "recollection" so dear to St. Teresa, and the "purity of heart" which Jesus assures us is blessed with the vision of God (Matt 5:8).

In this sense, attention is the key to contemplative meditation, attention to the here and now, the present reality of God within. "Remember how important it is to understand this truth," St. Teresa says, "that the Lord is within and that we should be there with him."[23] Thomas Merton expresses the same truth when he says:

> In prayer you discover what you already have through the indwelling Spirit of God and your incorporation through baptism into Christ...you start where you are and you deepen what you already have...all you need is to experience what you already possess.[24]

Through awareness, in loving attention, I allow my consciousness to be filled with the mystery of God as revealed in Jesus Christ. It is an attention that is alert yet still, gentle yet active, selfless yet involving the whole person. It is the prayer of someone fully alive to the glory and presence of God.

Prayer-Word

The link between presence and awareness in contemplative meditation is the prayer-word. This is the searchlight or the radar, as it were, that carries my awareness into the presence of God. The prayer-word or mantra is a love-word that helps to focus my attention on God and keep my mind from wandering. It is a short, simple, loving prayer spoken over and over again in the mind, in the heart and in the spirit. Not only has it got direction, it has power as well: power to deepen my awareness, power to create stillness and carry my attention into the deeper silence where God reveals himself beyond words, thoughts and images.

The New Testament is full of beautiful examples of prayer-words: "Lord, let me see" (Luke 18:41); "God, be merciful to me, a sinner!" (Luke 18:13); "Come, Lord Jesus!" (Rev 22:20). In his own prayer and in his teaching, Jesus gives us many prayer-words: "not my will but yours be done" (Luke 22:42); "into your hands I commend my spirit" (Luke

23:46); and each petition of the Our Father (Matt 6:9–13) are examples. The author of *The Cloud of Unknowing* speaks of the use of a "little word" and suggests a word of one syllable like "God" or "love."[25]

It is important to use a phrase or word that is short, simple and meaningful for you personally. Once you have found your prayer-word, all that is necessary is to say it slowly, with full attention and with love. You don't need to think a lot about it or to force meaning into it; rather, it should reveal its deeper meaning back to you. The name "Jesus," for example, or the phrase "My Lord and my God" (John 20:28) are compendiums of the whole gospel and can reveal ever deeper levels of meaning and insight. So as we say our prayer-word, first of all in our mind and then in our heart, we listen to the deeper vibrations of the Spirit speaking to us from within and drawing us more and more into silence.

PRAYER AND AWARENESS

God is present everywhere in the full capacity of His Existence. He cannot be more present to anyone by drawing closer or by bringing more of His Being into them. He becomes more present only in the sense that we can be put into fuller contact with Him: we become more alive and perceptive to His Presence as He meets us in a human way.[26]

—David Geraets, O.S.B.

The Zen master, Iyoko, was once asked by a disciple for a teaching. The master took a piece of paper and wrote on it the word "attention." Next day the disciple returned, saying that he did not understand what the master had written. Iyoko took the piece of paper again and wrote "attention, attention." The following day the disciple came back, still puzzled by the master's words. This time Iyoko wrote "attention, attention, attention."

The lesson the young disciple found it difficult to grasp is the oldest lesson in the world, the lesson of awareness and of total presence. It is the art of doing one thing at a time and living in the present moment. The past is past; we do not yet live in the future; and the only true focus of life is the present. Truth is not an abstraction; life is not a theory. If life is to be lived to the full, it can only be in the reality of the present moment.

Attentive Listening

To be attentive means to be present to something, to be aware and open to what is going on. We could speak of "concentration" if this did not conjure up images of wet towels, furrowed eyebrows and cramming for examinations! To concentrate, however, simply means to focus gently, yet positively, on what we are doing. For most of us this is not easy, since the normal span of human attentiveness is only twenty seconds! To live in the present moment is to experience life and not just to think about it. It is to let life teach us. We can spend so much time and energy imagining all sorts of possible situations, while all the time life itself is passing us by. The magic of the present moment eludes us because we are still trapped in the past or fearful of the future. Jesus directs us not to worry about tomorrow: "Today's trouble is enough for today" (Matt 6:34). The same advice could apply to the past as well.

The Right Time

The lesson Iyoko tried to teach his disciple is that same lesson that is often found in the lives of the saints. St. John Bosco, for example, was once playing billiards with some boys when one of them posed the question, "What would you do if the end of the world was announced?" Some were for going to the chapel, others to confession, while yet another said he would say his rosary. John Bosco, however, assured them that he would play his next shot! In the same way, St. Teresa of Avila once scandalized some of her Sisters who saw her eating partridge. But the saint calmly replied, "There is a time for penance and a time for partridge!"

Two thousand years before, the author of *Ecclesiastes* had already expressed the same idea:

> For everything there is a season,
> and a time for every matter under
>   heaven:…
> a time to weep,
> and a time to laugh;…
> a time to seek,
> and a time to lose;…
> a time to keep silence,
> and a time to speak. (Eccl 3:1,4, 6–7)

It is not that one season is better than another; it is simply that each has its own time. Playing billiards, eating partridge, being with friends, talking to God in prayer: each has its own season and each is right in its own time. The secret is not to compare one with another, but to enjoy each as it comes along. It is the same present moment that brings us the fellowship of our friends at table and the companionship of God at prayer. And if St. Teresa of Avila directed her nuns "not to talk to God and think about something else,"[27] you can be sure she would give exactly the same advice about talking to our friends.

Everything Is a Grace

Awareness, then, or attention as Iyoko called it, seems to be the key. But the key to attention is love. Love is the heart of presence. I am truly present only to the person I love. If I really love someone, I shall not be distracted out of their presence by other thoughts. This applies to other things as well: reading a good book, watching a film, taking a walk in the country. If I love what I am doing, then I am doing it with love.

To be attentive, then, means to be present. It means to see what is really happening, to

48

hear what is really being said. It is to experience rather than to project. It implies an attitude of receiving rather than controlling, of being gifted rather than achieving. It is to appreciate with humble reverence the little things as well as the great. It takes nothing for granted. To live in the present moment is not to impose a whole lot of thought and meaning on every event. It is, rather, to let the experience itself reveal its own inner meaning and for us to become humble disciples in the great school of life itself. "Everything is a grace," St. Thérèse of Lisieux once said[28]—and who knew better than she, who built her life upon the little experiences that came her way and transformed them by her love?

Stop—Look—Listen

Ultimately, then, we can only live in the present. We can plan for the future, we can learn from the past, but we can only live our lives in the reality of the present moment. Creative living means responding to the present situation. It is not a question of what may happen or what did happen, but of what *is* happening. And that's what matters. "Stop—Look—Listen" is not just good advice for children crossing the road. It is a guiding rule for all of us along the road of life: to *stop* the racing mind, the worried, anxious thoughts; to *look* attentively at what is really before us; and to *listen* to life as it comes to us moment by moment.

Strength and awareness come through presence as we learn to do one thing at a time. Of course, it is not really a question of doing one thing at a time; it is a matter of realizing that in fact that is all we *can* do! Most of the time, however, we try to do the impossible! We pressurize ourselves with a restless anxiety and feelings of hurry, and we never really give ourselves to the task at hand. The anxious mind teems with images of duties, obligations and responsibilities. So much to do and so little time to do it….Yet even in the busiest day, the countless tasks come one at a time.

Presence of God

Learning to live in the presence of God implies first of all learning to live in the present moment. God is not an abstraction. He is immediately and personally present to everything that is. If he is real, he is real here and now, whatever the circumstance, whatever the situation. If he is not in the present moment, he is nowhere.

God speaks to us in the things he has made, the everyday event, the people we meet. His presence is distilled moment by moment. Though he is infinitely present, it is in a finite mould. We glimpse his presence rather than grasp it: "we see in a mirror, dimly" (1 Cor 13:12), St. Paul puts it. Life both hides God and reveals him. The secret is to find life and let the presence reveal itself.

Learning to see the things God has made is one of the best ways of learning to see him. Being sensitive to the present reality makes us sensitive to the ultimate Reality. The chances are that I will never "see his blood upon the rose" if I do not first see the rose; the stars will never reveal "the glory of his eyes" if they do not first reveal their own.[29] In Matthew's Gospel, in the Last Judgment scene (Matt 25:31–46), those on the king's left hand were condemned not because they did not see Christ in others, but because they did not see the other—the sick, the hungry, the naked. Because they missed the present reality, they missed the reality of Christ.

God often hides himself in the obvious. Taking things for granted usually means taking *him* for granted as well. Yet he always remains the God of surprises and seems to delight in breaking into our dreary casualness in fresh and unexpected ways. This, ultimately, is the meaning of the New Testament: the scandal of the gospel. The helpless infant, the carpenter of Nazareth, the friend of sinners, the condemned man on the cross—they are, St. Paul reminds us, nothing less than "the glory of God in the face of Jesus Christ" (2 Cor 4:6). Jesus himself, in his own teaching, constantly recalls us not only to the reality of God, but to the God of Reality and the everyday things that reveal him: a mustard seed, a loaf of bread, wineskins and a widow's mite. It did not matter whether it was a wedding feast or a charcoal breakfast on the shore; those who had eyes to see saw his glory and believed (John 2:11). Perhaps this is why, in the Sermon on the Mount, Jesus tells us to look at the birds of the air and the lilies of the field (Matt 6:26–30). Look, really look, and they will point us to our Father's house.

PRAYER AND LIFE

I don't know Who—or what—put the question, I don't know when it was put, I don't even remember answering. But at some moment I did answer Yes to Someone—or Something—and from that hour I was certain that existence is meaningful and that, therefore, my life, in self-surrender, had a goal.
—Dag Hammarskjöld[30]

To pray is to let God into our lives. Prayer and life cannot be separated. If they are, prayer becomes unreal and life unsatisfying. Ultimately, the greatest prayer of all is not what we say, but what we do. The question is not whether we have "said" our prayers but whether we have lived them. Our deepest concern, then, should be to pray our lives, to make our lives the expression of our prayer. We should see prayer as the heartbeat of life which unites in one the hands of Martha with the heart of Mary (cf. Luke 10:38–42).

Response to Life

Prayer, in fact, can rightly be described as a response to life, a wholehearted and total saying "yes" to life and to God, the Author of life. To respond, however, means much more than simply replying with an indifferent "yes" or "no." It is a reply with a pledge in it: a commitment not just to think about life, but to live it as fully as possible so that our "yes" becomes fruitful and creative. Response implies responsibility, a choice freely made with open hands and open eyes. Saying "yes" to life is saying "yes" to God, the Living God who has called us to the fullness of life in his Son, Jesus Christ.

In every human situation we can respond either positively or negatively. We can face the challenge or we can withdraw from it. This applies to such everyday decisions as getting out of bed in the morning, answering the telephone or watching television. It covers the more important and challenging decisions like choosing a career, changing to a new job or deciding to emigrate. To each of these openings we can respond with a prayer or a complaint. Each of them can be a source of growth or of diminishment, a blessing or a curse. The glory of God is human beings fully alive, fully responsive, fully human. Holiness and wholeness are both variations on the same word, the same reality. True holiness always leads to and demands wholeness. The first purpose of prayer is not to make us better, but to make us more real, more authentic, more honest with God, with others and with ourselves. Then indeed it will make us better.

Walking in the Truth

The surest way to make prayer real is to begin with real life, to start with the concrete human situation in which we find ourselves. It is all too easy to slip into a daydream world with regard to prayer, to speak casually of an "elevation of the mind" or an "uplifting of the heart," as if this were the simplest thing in the world to do. Very often it is wiser to look at ourselves first and go to God through our needs. Whether we like it or not, the immediacy of our own everyday experience impinges on our consciousness, and for this reason it can be our first step in our response to God and to life.

This, perhaps, is the secret of such best-selling books over the years as Michel Quoist's *Prayers of Life*, Rita Snowdon's *A Woman's Book of Prayers*, and William Barclay's *The Plain Man's Book of Prayers*. A prayer is made out of the ordinary everyday events of life—a hospital ward, a telephone call, a letter from a friend or a football match. Whether it is at the kitchen sink or the supermarket, the city park or the subway station, a person reflects on life here and now, and so, out of the experience of the present moment, a prayer is made. The prayer can be one of joy and thanksgiving, of petition and supplication, or simply one of anguish and frustration. The circumstances shape the prayer and give it wings. This is surely what St. Paul meant when he urged his Christians to "pray in the Spirit at all times" (Eph 6:18).

To pray in this way means to base our prayer on truth. It means beginning with facts, not daydreams. It means accepting the truth about ourselves and about others: our homes and families, the office, the shop and the factory, the people we work with and those next door. In this way we come to God exactly as we are, spreading out our lives before him in humility and truth. It is basically what St. Teresa of Avila calls "walking in the truth."[31] We become like the men and women in the gospel who met Jesus in the circumstances of their daily lives. What else would a blind man ask for but to see, or a leper except to be made clean?

The Gift of Life

Finding God in the reality of life means, of course, facing up to life itself. Life itself is a challenge; it demands a response. But it is also a process, an invitation to growth and maturity, and prayer itself is part of this process, part of this becoming. God did not just create life, he *is* life, and he has shared this life with us. Something of himself is given to us in the gift of life. *I* live because *he* lives. To pray is to be aware of this mystery of life and this mystery of myself. Awareness is at the heart of *all* prayer—awareness of God as totally real and present to me, awareness of life itself as a gift, and awareness of myself as a unique and individual expression of God's creative and sustaining love. To reflect on life and search out its deeper meaning is ultimately to accept the invitation of the scriptures to "seek the face" of the living God (cf. Ps 24:6; Hos 5:15).

It is not just what I ask of life that is important, but what life asks of me. Life itself is given, it comes to me, and my essential response must always be a willingness to learn from it. To pray means both to ask questions and to hear them; to respond both by doing and by being. To pray does not mean to have all the answers to life; my prayer can be within the questions, within the searching and the seeking, even within the confusion and uncertainty that surround so much of my life. My response right now may be just to pray and live these questions, hoping one day to be able to hear and understand the answers. Prayer, like life itself, is a journey—but in each case the path is made by walking in it. "...those who do what is true," St. John reminds us, "come to the light" (John 3:21).

Providence

To "pray our lives" means to believe in God's caring providence. It means to see his guiding hand in all things, even the smallest events of our lives. To pray is to find God in our lives not only in the quiet moments of personal prayer, but also in the constant struggle and daily grind of workaday reality. Those who pray do not believe in accidents. There are no gaps in God's providence, no waste matter in his ruling of our lives. To the vision of faith all ground is holy ground, every bush is a burning bush (Exod 3:1–6). Events are the language of God; it is through them that he speaks to us whether in joy or in pain, in happiness or in sorrow. St. Thérèse of Lisieux understood this when she said, "Everything is a grace."[32]

To enter into God's providence is to enter into the present moment, the eternal "now." For it is in the here and now that God acts and that essentially he is to be found. This is what is meant when we say that for a Christian there is no tomorrow, only the given reality of the present moment. If we do not find God where we are, we may not find him at all; if we do not encounter him on earth, how can we meet him in heaven? Life itself is the first source of grace: God is within the ordinary, the trivial and the mundane. We can waste our time waiting for life to "happen," while all the time it is passing us by. Each moment, each event and each person is a God-given and God-bearing invitation to life and to love. Each is special because it is unique. How well Mary of Bethany understood this truth as she sat at the Lord's feet: the housework and the dishes would still be there tomorrow, but the present moment of Christ's visit was too precious to be distracted by anything but listening.

Prayer as Service

Yet prayer can never be an evasion of our responsibility or of our concern for other people. Life and prayer really become one when prayer issues forth in service; authentic prayer always increases self-giving. Someone has rightly said, "They pray badly who pray only on their knees." God asks for working hands as well as praying hands, hands to serve as well as hands to intercede.

61

Genuine service of others will force us back to prayer. Practical Christianity demands practical prayer. Caring for the sick, visiting the old, comforting the distressed, working for peace—these things cannot be done for God without his help. Thus, prayer becomes the workshop of life. In this sense, to work is to pray, but the prayer must already be in the heart; caring for others only makes it visible.

To say we have no time for prayer has no meaning if prayer and life are one. If we have time to live, we have time to pray! Prayer is not an optional extra; it is a way of living and a way of being. I can no more exclude life or others from my prayer than I can exclude God. Prayer is, in fact, my total response to God, to others and to myself. It is my sharing in God's creative and redemptive plan for the world. It is a call to life, a call to the fullness of that life which Christ came to share with us so abundantly.

PRAYER AND FRIENDSHIP

Prayer is very simply being on terms of friend-ship with God, frequently conversing alone with him who, we know, loves us.
                    —St. Teresa of Avila[33]

Prayer has been described as conversation with an ideal friend. Friendship is something that we all appreciate, and the idea of a perfect friend with whom we can communicate is certainly one that appeals to us.

Friendship is, in fact, an essential human experience. Few things in life are more precious. It is the one reality that dissolves loneliness and is a basic condition for any genuine human relationship or sharing. It is also a deeply religious experience—the vital atmosphere of our faith-response to God in prayer.

I Call You Friends

Most of us would find it hard enough to define friendship, but in practice we know what a real friend is. He or she is one with whom I can be totally myself and by whose presence in my life I am enriched. A friend is one with whom I can share thoughts and feelings, hopes and aspirations; one with whom I can share, without embarrassment, not only my tears and my laughter but also my silences. In a word, a friend is a friend not because of *what* I am, but just *because* I am.

Friendship is more than affection; its roots are deeper. It is more than fellowship; its bonds are closer. It may not be as great as love, but then love itself is dependent on it. We may not like those we love, but this distinction does not hold in friendship. We must like our friends, for friendship of its very nature is mutual; it either finds or makes persons equal. Perhaps this is what is meant by saying that it is not lack of love that upsets so many marriages, but lack of friendship.

The most essential quality of friendship is that it is creative. It brings out the best in me; without it, I would be less than I am. It is not that my friends do not know me as I am; true friendship is clear-sighted. But what a friend sees is what others miss—the miracle of me, so often hidden from myself. I rejoice not only in what my friend is in himself or herself, but also for what I am because of my friend.

Can you imagine the effect of our Lord's words to his disciples at the Last Supper: "I do not call you servants any longer,...I have called you friends" (John 15:15). Friends—*his* friends! From then on, everything was different. Humble fishermen, hated tax collectors—now they were the friends of Christ. He had seen the hidden possibilities and brought the miracle to light.

God Who Is Faithful

Prayer is friendship with God simply because God is a friend. This is how he has revealed himself. The God who walked with Adam and Eve in the garden in the cool of the evening (Gen 3:8), who spoke to Moses "face to face, as one speaks to a friend" (Exod 33:11), and who gathered Israel into the community of his chosen people, is the same God who calls us now to a new and eternal covenant of friendship with him. His friendship has stood the test of time and proved itself in countless ways; it is as everlasting and unchanging as God himself.

The whole meaning of the Christian revelation is that now, through grace, we are on terms of friendship with God. "Grace," St. Thomas Aquinas reminds us, "is nothing else but a certain friendship between God and ourselves."[34] And it is this gift of friendship that makes Christian prayer possible. "So then you are no longer strangers and aliens," St. Paul tells us, "but you are citizens with the saints and also members of the household of God" (Eph 2:19). We belong to the family of God, we are born of him: children of God at home in our Father's house.

Prayer, then, finds its full meaning as an expression of our friendship with God, and just to become aware of what this friendship really means is to break out automatically into prayer.

Conversation with a Friend

St. Teresa of Avila, a great teacher in the art of prayer, always saw prayer in terms of friendship with God: "Prayer is very simply being on terms of friendship with God, frequently conversing alone with him who, we know, loves us."[35] For St. Teresa, prayer is always a relationship of friendship, a mutual response in an atmosphere of openness and trust. She knew only too well that it is not just what we say to God that is important, but what we are before him.

To be true, then, prayer must reflect this friendly, intimate relationship with God. Our prayer should be easy, relaxed and spontaneous, without formality or constraint. We should not be shy or bashful with God, for that is to put up barriers to our friendship with him. It has often been said that the right way to talk to God is how a friend talks to a friend as they relax together in a chair before the fire!

But such a friendship is not easy, nor is it automatic. All friendship—human or divine—must be worked at and constantly renewed. Everyone needs friends, but unfortunately not everyone has them. The reason is simple: to have a friend, you must *be* one. People who won't take time and care to interest themselves in others can hardly expect friendships to grow and develop. Very often, real friendship is the fruit of sacrifice and demands an unselfish generosity that shows itself in confidence and trust. Our friendship with God is no exception: it must be kept in constant repair. But it is a friendship worth working at, and faithfulness and generosity in prayer are the foundations on which it is built.

Jesus Our Friend

Jesus spoke a lot about friendship. His own relationship with his disciples was a model for all human friendship: "I have called you friends, because I have made known to you everything I have learned from my Father" (John 15:15). For three years they were in his company, sharing the road, listening to his teaching and sitting down in table fellowship with him. They saw his miracles, shared the glory of Tabor, the agony in the garden and finally the joy of the resurrection.

Jesus knew the importance of friendship and mutual support among his disciples as he sent them out two by two to preach the Good News of the Kingdom. He knew, too, and appreciated the welcome he received in the house of his friends Martha and Mary, where he was obviously so much at home. Neither was Jesus ashamed to be called a "friend of sinners" (Luke 7:34), or to welcome them into his company. And when he wanted to express heaven's joy over a repentant sinner, he could find no better image than that of the father who killed the fatted calf and called together all his friends to rejoice with him and celebrate.

But it was above all in the Upper Room that the depths of Jesus' friendship were revealed. There, in that atmosphere of intimacy and familiarity, he laid bare his soul to his disciples. The Eucharist, the priesthood, the promise of the Spirit, the new commandment of love and the beautiful priestly prayer of Jesus all flowed together to be consummated ultimately on the cross when the "greater love" no one has was revealed and he "laid down his life for his friends" (see John 15:13). Thus, in his life and in his death, Jesus revealed to his disciples and to all his followers down through the ages the nature of our relationship with God—a relationship of friendship, sharing and love that is ultimately the root and foundation that makes all prayer possible.

Friendship with Others

Just as we can learn a lot about human friendship from Jesus, so we can learn a lot about friendship with God from our relationship with others. Every true human friendship is a mirror of the divine and points to it. God does a lot of his loving of us through other people and gives us the chance to return his love in the same way. The disciples on the road to Emmaus met Christ as they went along sharing the road together. Though they were dejected and downcast and their whole world had fallen about their ears, yet they remained together; they had each other; and in that fellowship they found the Risen Lord (Luke 24:13–32). How often does Christ come along the way of human friendship to walk the road of life with us!

In friendship, one human life is taken hold of by another. In prayer, that other is God. Prayer, like friendship, can never be abstract or theoretical—it has its roots in each one's personal discovery of God and individual relationship with him.

Words are not the most important element in friendship, neither are they in prayer. The soul of friendship is sharing, being together, rejoicing in each other's presence. Prayer, too, is not so much talking to God as sharing his presence. When we pray we deepen our awareness of this presence; we make it more real and active. Certainly, in prayer absence does not make the heart grow fonder! To grow in prayer is to grow in friendship with God. In him all friendship finds its source. Prayer renews our weary souls in the spring of his eternal friendship.

PRAYER OF PETITION

We do not express our needs to God either to inform God of what he does not know or to persuade God to change his mind. If we pray for our needs it is above all because doing so deepens our trust that God knows and God cares....In silence we accept that God knows our needs and that this knowledge is the love which creates and will eventually complete us.
—Laurence Freeman, O.S.B.[36]

For many people, prayer simply means asking things of God. This is perhaps the most common and accepted understanding of prayer. Certainly it finds every encouragement in the scriptures where we are told to present our needs to God, asking in faith and trusting in his goodness. St. Paul's directions are explicit: "...in everything by prayer and supplication with thanksgiving let your requests be made known to God" (Phil 4:6).

Our God is a God who gives. He likes giving and wants to share his gifts with us. As God and Father, he is attentive to our needs. This is the foundation of all prayer and the basis of our confidence. This is the meaning of St. John's saying "God is love" (1 John 4:8)—a meaning caught very beautifully in a saying attributed to St. Teresa of Avila: "He knows all things, he can do all things and he loves me."

Afraid to Ask

Most people pray in times of great distress or in a crisis. "There are no atheists on a life raft" was a saying of World War II. When all human help seemed lost, men and women raised their eyes to heaven and prayed. God may not be the "god of the gaps," but it is often only in the "gaps," when we come to the end of our own strength, that we begin to acknowledge God's.

Yet prayer is surely more than a last resort, a desperate cry for help when all else has failed. Asking God for help means more than turning to him when we have reached the end of our own resources. The truth is that as long as we live in this valley of tears, our constant approach to God must be that of persons in need. We are wayfarers journeying the road of life, carrying ourselves, as St. Paul reminds us, "in clay jars" (2 Cor 4:7). For the blessed in heaven, their normal prayer may be one of praise; for us who are travelers on the way, more often it is the prayer of petition. That is why St. Thomas Aquinas, writing about prayer, defined it as "asking God for things that are right and fitting."[37] Simply to ask is to admit our need, our helplessness, our poverty. Prayer is not a matter of hiding our littleness but of presenting it to God in order to receive his healing love and mercy. Our fundamental attitude toward God must always be one of honesty. Prayer is not only a call for help; it is first and foremost an acknowledgment that everything we are and everything we have comes from God.

Nor is it true to say that, since God knows our needs, it is not necessary to ask him. Prayer is not a matter of telling God something he does not know, but rather a way of reminding ourselves of something we so easily forget—that God is God and we are dependent on him. When we ask God for something, we bring into the open our real relationship with him: we acknowledge this truth about God and about ourselves. We cannot hide our hearts from God, nor should we try to do so. Rather, as we accept our brokenness and littleness, we make space within our hearts to receive his healing grace.

The Our Father

When the disciples asked Jesus to teach them to pray, he taught them the Our Father which is one continuous prayer of petition. He taught them to ask for many things: the coming of the Kingdom, the fulfillment of God's will and the everyday necessities of life—daily bread, pardon for faults and deliverance from evil. The Our Father is the prayer of persons fully conscious of their fundamental relationship with God, people with their feet firmly on the ground and their faces set steadfastly toward God.

In the gospels we see how Jesus' personal prayer was a reflection of everything he taught his disciples. Many times he turned confidently to his Father in prayer: he prayed with the little children, at the tomb of Lazarus, and for Peter that his "faith may not fail" (Luke 22:32). Chapter 17 of John's Gospel gives perhaps the most beautiful example of Jesus' own prayer. This prayer is quite remarkable both in its detail and in the number of things for which he prayed. His prayer was personal (he prayed for those who were listening to him, for their unity, their safety, their joy), and yet it was wide enough to embrace all people down through the ages who "will believe in me through their word" (John 17:20).

So there is nothing humiliating or demeaning about the prayer of petition. God is our Father and we are never more fully his children than when we turn to him in confident prayer. We stand before him as persons, free and independent, simply acknowledging our own need and his power to help. Indeed, by unveiling ourselves before him, we enter into his creative designs for us; we share, as instruments, in his gentle government of the world.

A God Who Cares

Underlying all prayer of petition there must be a firm belief in the providence of God, a strong awareness that God is very much present and active in this world of ours. He is at the innermost heart of all reality, powerfully accomplishing his purpose. He is not an absentee landlord or a remote-control officer. He is present to and within his own creation, intimately involved in all that concerns this world of flesh and blood. This does not mean that God acts wantonly or interferes at random in his own universe. He is the first to respect the laws he himself has made, just as he is the first to honor the freedom and independence he has given us. But it does mean that God cares for each of us, knows us by name and is always moved to order things creatively for our good: "Look at the birds of the air," Jesus said, "...Are you not more precious than any of these?" (Matt 6:26).

Every prayer of petition, then, implies an act of faith in the reality of God's presence, a presence that is both immediate and active. It is easy enough to see God's hand in the pleasant things of life. It is not so easy to see it in the more difficult and painful things. And yet "for those who love God all things work together for good" (Rom 8:28). St. Augustine, reflecting on these words of St. Paul in the light of his own experience, added, "yes, even our sins." God is the infinitely consummate artist who "writes straight with crooked lines," bringing good out of evil, beauty out of chaos, and changing Good Friday into Easter Sunday morning.

Unanswered Prayer

Many people are distressed by the problem of unanswered prayer. They feel somehow that their prayers should have a magic power to achieve what they ask. They forget the simple fact that some prayers are impossible even for God, either because of the nature of the request or because God loves us too much to grant them. What mother will give her child a knife to play with or let it walk unattended on a busy street, no matter how much the child wants to do so? The truth is that God always answers our prayers with an eye on eternity. He sees beyond the passing need to something deeper and greater. After all, the object of all prayer is to lay hold of God himself and not just his answers. It is not what God gives that we need, so much as God himself. "I am the ground of your beseeching," God reminded Julian of Norwich.[38]

Someone has rightly said that God answers every prayer—sometimes the answer is "yes," sometimes it is "no," sometimes it is "wait." And it is the waiting, above all, that tests our faith.

In the scriptures there are many examples of unanswered prayers. Moses prayed to enter the Promised Land and his prayer was not granted. David prayed unavailingly for the life of his child. Paul, too, was refused when he asked to be freed from the "thorn in the flesh" (2 Cor 12:7). Perhaps the strangest refusal of all was in Gethsemane when Jesus asked that the chalice might pass him by. He who said, "Ask, and it will be given to you" (Matt 7:7), did ask and it was not given. At least not then: even Jesus had to wait. Three days later his prayer was answered.

Prayer Answered

There are many prayers God wants us to answer ourselves! When we say "thy will be done," we mean not only by God, but by us as well, here and now. Indeed, many of our prayers are already answered before we make them. By keeping God's commandments and living our Christian faith, we already have the solution to many of our troubles and worries.

It is sometimes said that instead of praying for people, we should do something for them. Instead of praying for the hungry, we should feed them; instead of interceding for the sick, we should nurse them. But one does not exclude the other, and the God to whom we pray is also the source of all food and health and life. At the same time, genuine prayer is always a spur to action. I can hardly pray with full earnestness for another in need if I am not prepared to do everything I can in a practical way to help. St. Thomas More, the 16th-century English martyr, expressed this truth very beautifully in one of his favorite prayers: "The things I pray for, Lord, give me the grace to work for."[39]

There is nothing too small or too unimportant to bring to God in prayer. The golden rule stands: if it is something I can honestly wish for, then I can just as earnestly pray for it. Indeed, it is a good habit to ask God for little things, becoming, as the gospel invites us, as little children, casting all our care upon the Lord (Matt 18:3; 1 Pet 5:7). Often it is our own sense of importance, not God's, that keeps us from humble, childlike prayer to him.

But in the end, of course, our prayer will be one of gratitude—gratitude that God himself, in his wisdom, sorted out all our requests. For the chances are that, as they stood, they could well have increased our sorrows rather than our joys.

PRAYER AND COMPASSION

Christ has no body now on earth but yours,
no hands but yours,
no feet but yours.
Yours are the eyes through which looks out
Christ's compassion on the world.
Yours are the feet with which
Christ is to go about doing good.
Yours are the hands with which
he is to bless people today.
                    —Words attributed
                    to St. Teresa of Avila

Two friends were once fighting in the same battalion close to the enemy line when one of them failed to return. The other asked for permission to go out and look for him. But the officer did not want him to risk his life as his friend was probably dead. Nevertheless the other went and returned a short while later, mortally wounded and carrying the body of his dead friend. The officer was furious: "I told you he was dead; now I've lost both of you. Was it worth going out to bring in a corpse?" "Yes," the dying man replied, "when I got there he was still alive and his last words were, 'I knew you'd come.'"

Sometimes the best prayers are not the ones we say but the ones we *do*. In fact, sometimes they may not seem to us to be prayers at all; but any action born out of love is in itself a prayer. A compassionate heart cannot help expressing itself in deeds of love and, whether aware of it or not, walks along the way of prayer.

A Way of Love

Prayer that excludes others is not Christian prayer. Real prayer always has an outward dimension to it. Though it springs from within, its effects flow out to other people. Prayer must touch not only the lips but also the heart and hands; it must express itself in action as well as in words. As St. Teresa said, she would not give much for the sort of prayer that is always turned inwards and thinks only of itself.[40] True prayer is born out of compassion. Compassion—not in the sense of pity or even sympathy, but in its deepest sense of sharing with and entering into the "passion" of another human being. To say, "I'll pray for you" is one thing; to witness to the reality of that prayer in deeds of love is, in fact, the test.

Togetherness

Compassion is not just a feeling *for* someone; it is much more a feeling *with*—a oneness, a togetherness, an empathy. It is neither sacrificial nor vicarious; it neither gives nor takes. It simply *is*. It is much more a question of being than of doing: a reaching out and into another person's experience in order to make it one's own.

The root of compassion is solidarity, the basic reality of our shared human experience. At the deepest level, what we hold in common—that strange, wonderful thing we call "our human nature"—is a vast reservoir of common thoughts, feelings and emotions. We are all so much alike—full of boundless hopes, dreams and promises—yet all the while hurt, wounded and scarred. The same current runs through the blood of all of us: fear and joy, laughter and sorrow, tears and smiles. There is no human response that I experience today that someone else will not experience tomorrow or has not already done—no fear or worry, no joy or happiness for which there is not some human common denominator.

We are all, in a sense, incomplete. We need others just as much as they need us. We belong to others just as much as we belong to ourselves. The "other" is part of me. To know another human being and enter into his or her passion is to awaken within myself the agony and the ecstasy of our shared human condition.

The Way of Tenderness

Compassion is concerned with feelings, not with ideas or insights. It means putting oneself in another person's shoes, wearing the same clothes, feeling the same feelings, sharing the same emotions. Compassion moves along the way of tenderness, yet it enters into the whole world of human reality: fear, loneliness, rejection, despair, sometimes even the ultimate despair—despair of life itself.

Compassion takes what it finds—the raw, brute reality of each human experience. It is not concerned with "problems" but with people, or rather with the one unique human being with whom it seeks to identify. Compassion does not seek to solve, even when a solution is obvious, or to argue when a situation is negative. It does not need to judge, give advice or offer directions. It is not afraid of silence, or of tears or of laughter. Rather, it is a quality of offering to another human being a free space and a safe boundary within which they can feel at home.

Perhaps, in the end, it is the difference, in a rescue situation, between throwing a rope down the well and going down into the well oneself.

A Compassionate God

In the scriptures, God has shown himself as a God of mercy and compassion. To Moses on Mount Sinai he revealed himself as "a God merciful and gracious, slow to anger, and abounding in steadfast love and faithfulness" (Exod 34:6). Unlike the gods of the surrounding nations, Israel's God was a personal God, one who had come into their lives working "signs and wonders" (Heb 2:4) as he led them out of slavery, through the desert and into their own land. He was a God close to his people; he revealed his name to them, fought their battles, healed their wounds, and carried them "on eagles' wings" (Exod 19:4). He was their God and they were his people.

But there was a still greater revelation to come. In Jesus we see the fullness of God's compassion, God truly "with us" (Matt 1:23, 28:20), having a human face and a human heart, sharing our flesh and blood. Now God himself was a partner and a companion in our human condition—weak, vulnerable, fragile. Like us "in every respect," (cf. Heb 4:15) we are told, especially the things that make us most human: our tears and laughter, our fears and joys, our hopes and disappointments. This was compassion in its truest sense, a sharing in the whole broken, fragile world of human reality.

Time and time again we see him "moved with compassion" (Matt 20:34; Mark 1:41), either for the multitude or for the individual who came to him: the leper, the blind man, the woman caught in adultery, the thief on the cross. They recognized him as one of themselves; they knew his tears were just as remarkable as his miracles.

Prayer of the Heart

It is out of this sort of compassion that true prayer is born. If prayer is turning to God, it is also a turning toward others, identifying with them as we walk the road of life together. Real prayer has no boundaries of race, language or creed. It sees only a brother or sister, someone with whom we share a mutual struggle and a mutual destiny. Across the barriers of language or land we are all one, and in that oneness we find the heart of God and the heart of all our fellow travelers. They are all there: those who seek the truth and those who are afraid of it, those who walk in the light and those who worship from afar, those who love and those who are unable to receive love.

Mahatma Gandhi saw prayer as "the daily admission of our weakness." Compassionate prayer is surely the daily admission of our corporate weakness, the humble acknowledgement of our need for each other as much as our need for God. Prayer makes us stop and listen; it invites us to pay attention and be aware. If I listen to my own heart, I am listening to the heart of all men and all women, and when I hear the "cry of the poor" I am admitting my own poverty and my own helplessness. When the only son of an elderly widow was killed, the Curé of Ars came to visit her. People expected the saintly Curé would somehow make sense of such a terrible tragedy. But all he could do was to sit there in silence with his arms around her and let his tears flow with her own.

To pray for other people is not a subtle effort to influence the will of God. Rather, it is to invite them into our own hearts and make their needs our own. To pray for others means to make them part of ourselves. It is not just a question of "remembering" a sick friend, an unemployed neighbor or a distressed relative, but somehow of "becoming" those for whom I pray. I stand with them before the face of God and my prayer becomes theirs and their cry becomes mine. Together we place ourselves and our needs before our Father and open our hearts to the healing power of his Spirit.

Compassionate prayer is corporate prayer. It is a way of being together, an expression of fellowship and of shared faith. It is the cry of all who suffer: the prisoner, the exile, the victim of war, violence or injustice, the forgotten. But it is also the praise of those who celebrate: christening robes, wedding bells and examinations passed are all part of a common joy and happiness we share together. Compassionate prayer binds and heals; it unites in suffering and in thanksgiving and makes the world a very small place of welcome and hospitality. It is the pilgrim prayer of a pilgrim people.

In the end, compassion is love and prayer is love. And they are both one.

Notes

1. Cf. *Autobiography of a Saint*, chapter XXXVII (Knox translation).
2. *Living Flame of Love*, 3:28.
3. *Autobiography of a Saint*, chapter XXXVII (Knox translation).
4. *Chapters*, 113, quoted in Kallistos Ware, *The Power of the Name: The Jesus Prayer in Orthodox Spirituality* (Oxford: SLG Press, 1974), p. 2.
5. *Way of Perfection*, 21:5.
6. *Living Flame of Love*, 3:59.
7. *Way of Perfection*, 17:2.
8. Cf. Roger Hudleston, O.S.B. (ed.), *The Spiritual Letters of Dom John Chapman*, O.S.B., (London: Sheed & Ward, 1935), p. 25.
9. *Autobiography of a Saint*, chapter XXXVII (Knox translation).

10. *Le Milieu Divin: An Essay on the Interior Life* (London: Collins, 1960), pp. 36–7.
11. *Spiritual Canticle*, stanza 5.
12. *Revelations of Divine Love*, chapter 5.
13. Based on a phrase attributed to St. Augustine: cf. St. Teresa of Avila, *Life*, 40:6, and *Way of Perfection*, 28:2.
14. *The Practice of the Presence of God* (New York: Image Books, 1977), p. 68.
15. *Way of Perfection*, 28:5.
16. Cf. letter 9 [sometimes letter 4], to an unnamed woman, c.1689.
17. *Way of Perfection*, 24:5.
18. Malcolm Muggeridge, *Something Beautiful for God: Mother Teresa of Calcutta* (London: Collins, 1971), p. 66.
19. See note 13.
20. *Christian Meditation: Prayer in the Tradition of John Cassian* (Alvaston: The Grail, 1978), p. 11.
21. *Interior Castle*, IV.1:7.
22. *Way of Perfection*, 28:2.
23. Ibid., 28:3.
24. David Steindl-Rast, "Recollection of Thomas Merton's Last Days in the West." Cf. *Monastic Studies*, 7 (1969), pp. 2–3.
25. *Cloud of Unknowing*, chapter 7.
26. *Jesus Beads* (New Mexico: Dove Publications, 1972), p. 15.
27. *Way of Perfection*, 22:8.

28. *Last Conversations*, "The Yellow Notebook," 5 June 1897, # 4.

29. Joseph Mary Plunkett, "I see His Blood upon the Rose," in *The Oxford Book of English Mystical Verse* (Oxford: Clarendon Press, 1917), p. 561.

30. *Markings* (London: Faber & Faber, 1975), p. 169.

31. *Interior Castle*, VI.10:7.

32. See note 28.

33. *Life*, 8:5.

34. Cf. *Summa Theologica,* IIa IIae, q. 23, art. 1.

35. See note 33.

36. *Christian Meditation: Your Daily Practice* (Alresford: Hunt & Thorpe, 1994), p. 14.

37. *Summa Theologica*, IIa IIae, q. 83, art. 5 (quoting St. John Damascene).

38. *Revelations of Divine Love*, chapter 41.

39. Cf. *English Prayers and Treatise on the Holy Eucharist by St Thomas More* (London: Burns Oates & Washbourne, 1938), p. 20.

40. Cf. *Way of Perfection*, 3:6-7.